Copyrighted Mate

CW00971702

# CANADA TRAVEL GUIDE 2023

Ultimate Tips for visiting to help you save time, money, and stress when planning your Canada vacation.

## BY

Alexander A

Copyrighted Material

# Copyright page

ALL rights reserved. No part of this publication may be reproduced, distributed, or transmitted in any form or by any means, including photocopying, recording, or other electronic or mechanical methods, without the prior written permission of the publisher, except in the case of brief quotations embodied in critical reviews and certain other noncommercial uses permitted by copyright law.
Copyright ©**Alexander A,** (2023).

Copyrighted Material

## Table of contents

Copyrighted Material

Copyrighted Material

## Chapter 1

## Welcome to canada

Canada is a country in the northern part of North America. It is the world's second-largest country by total area, with a population of over 37 million people. Canada is a federal parliamentary democracy and a constitutional monarchy, with Queen Elizabeth II as its head of state. Canada is made up of 10 provinces and three territories and is divided into two official languages: English and French.

Copyrighted Material

Canada is one of the world's most diverse countries, with a variety of cultures, languages, and religions represented. The country is known for its natural beauty and vast wilderness areas, which are home to a wide variety of wildlife. Canada is also a major trading partner with the United States and is a member of the United Nations, the G8, and the Commonwealth of Nations.

Canada is home to a variety of cultures and ethnicities. The country is home to the original inhabitants of the land, the First Nations, Inuit, and Métis peoples, as well as a large number of immigrants from around the world. The country is also home to a large population of French-speaking Canadians, many of whom have lived in Canada for generations.

Copyrighted Material

Canada is a major economic power in the world, with a strong and diversified economy based on natural resources, manufacturing, and services. Canada is a leading exporter of natural resources such as timber, oil, and natural gas. The country is also a leader in the production of many manufactured goods, including automobiles and aerospace products. Canada has a strong tourism industry, with millions of visitors every year.

Canada is a country of great contrasts, with a wide range of climates, landscapes, and cultures. It is a country with a rich and varied history, and its citizens are proud of their nation and its place in the world.

A visit to Canada is an unforgettable experience that will give you a chance to experience the country's immense beauty, friendly people, and vibrant culture. Canada

Copyrighted Material

is a great place to explore, and its people will welcome you with open arms.

Canada is truly an amazing place, and one that you won't soon forget.

## LOCATION

Canada is the world's second-largest country by total area, occupying most of northern North America. It is a federal parliamentary democracy and a constitutional monarchy, with Queen Elizabeth II being the head of state. Its ten provinces and three territories extend from the Atlantic to the Pacific and northward into the Arctic Ocean, covering 9.98 million square kilometers (3.85 million square miles), making it the world's second-largest country by total area.

Canada is bordered by the United States to the south and northwest. Canada stretches

Copyrighted Material

from the Atlantic Ocean in the east to the Pacific Ocean in the west; to the north lies the Arctic Ocean. Greenland is to the northeast and the Atlantic Ocean to the east. Canada is the world's most northernly country, and it is home to the world's longest coast line.

Canada has a highly diverse landscape, ranging from its mountainous regions in the west to the prairies in the east, and from the boreal forests in the north to the temperate rainforests of the British Columbia coast. Canada's climate is highly varied, ranging from the coldest winter temperatures in the world in the northern territories to the moderated summers of the prairies.

Canada is home to a variety of cultures and ethnicities, and is officially bilingual in both English and French. It has a rich history, and is known for its vibrant arts

Copyrighted Material

scene, strong economy, and beautiful natural landscapes.

Canada is a popular destination for tourists, with its diverse attractions such as its natural beauty, cultural attractions, and vibrant cities. It is also home to some of the world's most spectacular national parks, including Banff National Park, Jasper National Park, and Yoho National Park.

Canada is a country of opportunity, offering its citizens a high quality of life, a stable political system, and a healthy environment. It is a peaceful and welcoming nation, and its diverse population makes it an ideal destination for people of all backgrounds.

Canada is a great place to live, work, study, and visit. With its vibrant cities, expansive natural beauty, and welcoming people, Canada is a world-class destination for those looking for a new home or a vacation spot.

Copyrighted Material

From its majestic mountain peaks to its vast prairies, from its sparkling lakes to its winding rivers, Canada is truly a land of wonder and beauty.

Whether you're looking for a place to call home, a place to explore, or a place to simply relax, Canada has something for everyone.

From its vibrant cities to its vast wilderness, Canada is a land of opportunity and adventure. Come explore all that Canada has to offer.

The history of Canada dates back thousands of years, to the time of the first Indigenous peoples. Archaeological evidence shows that these peoples lived in Canada for at least 10,000 years. Over the centuries, these peoples developed a variety of cultures, languages and traditions. In the early 1500s, Europeans began to explore the eastern part of North America. The first Europeans to

Copyrighted Material

arrive in what is now Canada were French traders and explorers, followed by French settlers. The French established a number of settlements, particularly in Quebec and the Maritimes. In the 1700s, Britain and France fought a series of wars for control of North America. In 1763, Britain won the Seven Years' War and took control of Canada. The British then began to encourage immigration from Britain and other parts of the world, leading to a large influx of settlers. In 1867, the provinces of Canada, New Brunswick and Nova Scotia joined together to form the Dominion of Canada. Over the following decades, more provinces and territories joined the Dominion, resulting in the Canada we know today. Since Confederation, Canada has become an independent nation with a strong economy and a vibrant culture. It is a leader in the international community and is recognized

Copyrighted Material

for its commitment to diversity, equality and human rights. The history of Canada is filled with stories of courage, resilience and achievement. It is a story of immigrants and Indigenous peoples, of diverse cultures, languages and traditions. It is a story of a nation that is constantly striving to be better. Today, Canada is a vibrant, multicultural country, with a rich and proud history.

## Climate

Canada's climate varies widely from region to region. In general, the country has four distinct seasons. Summers are usually warm, with temperatures reaching up to 30°C (86°F) in some areas. Winters are

Copyrighted Material

cold, with temperatures often dropping below -20°C (-4°F).

The country's western regions experience the highest levels of precipitation, while the east experiences the lowest. The Prairies region experiences hot, dry summers and cold winters, while the Pacific Coast region has mild winters and cool summers. The northern regions of the country experience long, cold winters and short, cool summers.

Canada also experiences extreme weather events, such as tornadoes, blizzards, and hurricanes. The country is prone to flooding during the spring thaw, which occurs when snow and ice melts after the winter months.

Canada's climate is changing due to global warming. Temperatures in the country are expected to increase over the coming years, resulting in more extreme weather events.

Copyrighted Material

Canada has four distinct seasons. Summers are typically warm, with temperatures reaching up to 30°C (86°F) in some areas. Winters are cold, with temperatures often dropping below -20°C (-4°F). Canada experiences extreme weather events, such as tornadoes, blizzards, and hurricanes. The country is also prone to flooding during the spring thaw.

The climate in Canada varies greatly depending on the region. The Prairies region experiences hot, dry summers and cold winters, while the Pacific Coast region has mild winters and cool summers. The northern regions of the country experience long, cold winters and short, cool summers.

Due to global warming, temperatures in Canada are expected to increase over the coming years, resulting in more extreme weather events. This could have a significant impact on the country's climate, with more

Copyrighted Material

floods, droughts, and other extreme weather events becoming more common.

Copyrighted Material

## Chapter 2

## Popular Tourist Sites in Canada

Tourist Sites in Canada Canada is a vast and diverse country with many exciting attractions for tourists. From the magnificent Rocky Mountains in the west to the breathtaking Bay of Fundy in the east, there is something for everyone to explore and enjoy. Popular tourist sites in Canada include Niagara Falls, the CN Tower in Toronto, Banff National Park, and the world-famous Calgary Stampede. Other attractions include Quebec City, Old Montreal, Butchart Gardens in Victoria, the Canadian Museum of History in Ottawa, and the Whistler Blackcomb ski resort in British Columbia. No matter where you go, you're sure to find something to make your trip to Canada unforgettable.

Copyrighted Material

## Niagara Falls

Niagara Falls is a group of three waterfalls located on the border between Canada and the United States. It is comprised of the Horseshoe Falls, American Falls and Bridal Veil Falls. It is one of the most recognizable and powerful waterfalls in the world, and is a popular tourist destination. The Horseshoe Falls is the largest of the three falls, and is situated on the Canadian side. It is around 2,600 feet wide and has a drop of around 170 feet. It is considered the most powerful waterfall in North America, with a flow rate of up to 6 million cubic feet per minute. The American Falls is located on the American side of the border, and is around 1,000 feet wide. It has a drop of around 70 feet and has a flow rate of around 4 million cubic feet per minute. The Bridal Veil Falls

Copyrighted Material

is the smallest of the three falls, and is located on the American side. It is around 600 feet wide and has a drop of around 50 feet. It has a flow rate of around 1.5 million cubic feet per minute. The Niagara River is the source of the water for the waterfalls, and is around 35 miles long. It starts at Lake Erie and ends at Lake Ontario. The Niagara Gorge is a 12-mile-long and 1,200-foot-deep gorge that was created by thousands of years of erosion from the Niagara River. The falls were formed during the last Ice Age, around 12,000 years ago. As the glaciers melted they created the Niagara River, and the river eroded the rock at the base of the falls and created the three waterfalls. Niagara Falls is one of the most popular tourist destinations in the world, and attracts millions of visitors every year. It is a popular spot for sightseeing, and there are several observation decks, boat tours and other

Copyrighted Material

attractions that offer visitors a unique view of the falls. The falls are also a major source of hydroelectric power for the region, and provides power to millions of people. It is also home to several species of birds, fish and other wildlife. Niagara Falls is an awe-inspiring sight, and is a testament to the power of nature. It is a powerful force of nature that has captivated people for centuries, and continues to draw people from all over the world to witness its beauty. From its impressive size and power, to its unique history and wildlife, Niagara Falls is a natural wonder that is sure to leave a lasting impression.

## CN Tower

The CN Tower is a communications and observation tower in downtown Toronto, Ontario, Canada. Standing at a height of 553.3 metres (1,815 ft 5 in), it was the tallest

Copyrighted Material

free-standing structure in the world from 1976 until 2007 when it was surpassed by the Burj Khalifa in Dubai. The CN Tower is the symbol of Toronto, and a landmark of Canada. The CN Tower was built between 1973 and 1976 by Canadian National Railway, to serve as a telecommunications hub. The tower was designed by Canadian engineer John Andrews, and was constructed of steel and concrete. It is composed of three main tubular sections, which are connected by structural steel and concrete floors. At the top of the tower is a large observation deck, which provides panoramic views of the city. The CN Tower is also home to the world's highest indoor observation deck, the SkyPod, at 447 metres (1,465 ft). The SkyPod is a three-storey glass-enclosed observation deck, with a 360-degree view of the city. The CN Tower also features two restaurants, the 360

Copyrighted Material

Restaurant and the Horizons Café, both of which offer stunning views of the city. The CN Tower is also a popular tourist attraction The CN Tower also features an interactive museum and a glass floor where visitors can stand and look straight down at the street below. On the outside of the tower, visitors can take a ride in a glass-enclosed elevator, which takes them up to the observation deck. There are also two observation decks, the LookOut Level at 346 metres (1,135 ft), and the SkyPod at 447 metres (1,465 ft). The CN Tower also hosts many special events, such as the EdgeWalk. The EdgeWalk is a thrilling event in which visitors are strapped into a harness and allowed to walk around the circumference of the tower's main observation deck, at a height of 356 metres (1,168 ft). In addition to its many attractions, the CN Tower is also an important communications hub. The tower

Copyrighted Material

is equipped with powerful antennas, which are used for radio and television broadcasting, cellular telephone services, and satellite communications. The tower is also used to transmit data for business, government, military and consumer services. The CN Tower is also a popular tourist destination, attracting over two million visitors each year. The CN Tower is an iconic structure that has become an integral part of the skyline of Toronto. It stands as a symbol of Canada's engineering and technological prowess, and is a lasting testament to the city's spirit and determination. The CN Tower is a landmark of Toronto and Canada. It stands tall in the city, a symbol of Canadian pride and strength. It is a beacon of technological advancement and a testament to the power of human ingenuity. It is a place that offers a unique perspective of the city below, and an

Copyrighted Material

opportunity to experience the beauty of Toronto from a unique vantage point. The CN Tower is a must-see for any visitor to Toronto, and a reminder of the city's proud history and bright future. The CN Tower is a source of pride for Canadians and an iconic symbol of the city of Toronto. It stands tall in the skyline, and its distinctive shape is recognized around the world. It is a symbol of progress and of human achievement, and it stands as a reminder of how far we have come and how much more we can accomplish. The CN Tower is a symbol of what it means to be Canadian and a lasting reminder of our engineering prowess and technological advancement. The CN Tower is a source of pride and joy for all Canadians, and it stands as a testament to the power of human ingenuity.

Copyrighted Material

## Banff National Park

Banff National Park is a Canadian national park located in the Canadian Rockies in Alberta, Canada. It is Canada's oldest national park, established in 1885. The park encompasses 6,641 square kilometers of mountainous terrain, with numerous glaciers, icefields, alpine meadows, and dense forest. Mount Rundle and Cascade Mountain are the two most prominent peaks in the park. The park is home to a wide variety of wildlife, including grizzly and black bears, bighorn sheep, elk, deer, moose, wolves, wolverines, and many species of birds and fish. It is also home to the world's largest land mammal, the bison. Banff National Park offers a wide variety of activities for visitors, including camping, hiking, biking, horseback riding, wildlife watching, fishing, and skiing. The park is

Copyrighted Material

also home to over 1,500 kilometers of trails, ranging from easy to difficult, which provide excellent opportunities for exploration. The park is a popular destination for visitors from around the world, and its unique landscape, stunning views, and abundant wildlife make it a must-see destination for any traveler. The nearby town of Banff offers numerous accommodations, restaurants, and shopping opportunities, and is a great place to base your visit to the park. Banff National Park is an incredible place to explore and experience the beauty of the Canadian Rockies. Its stunning landscape, abundant wildlife, and wealth of activities make it a great destination for anyone looking to experience the best of the Canadian outdoors.

Copyrighted Material

## Chapter 3

## Transportation in Canada

Transportation in Canada is essential to its economy and way of life. Canada has a vast network of roads, railways, and waterways that enable goods and services to move freely throughout the country. The country also has a highly developed air transportation system, which is a critical part of the country's infrastructure. Canada also has several major ports that serve as gateways to international trade. In addition, the country has an extensive public transportation system, which includes buses, subways, light rail, and commuter trains. All of these transportation systems are essential to the country's economic growth and development. Canada's strong transportation infrastructure has allowed

Copyrighted Material

the country to become a major player in international trade. The country's key ports, such as Vancouver and Halifax, have been instrumental in allowing Canada to take advantage of global markets. In addition, the Canadian government has invested heavily in modernizing the country's transportation infrastructure, which is helping to reduce congestion and improve efficiency. Canada's transportation infrastructure also plays an important role in tourism, as it helps to make the country an attractive destination for visitors from around the world. Overall, transportation in Canada is an essential part of the country's infrastructure and economy. The country's extensive network of roads, railways, and waterways, as well as the highly developed air transportation system, are essential to the movement of goods and services and the continued development of the country.

Copyrighted Material

Canada's strong transportation infrastructure and investment in modernizing it have been instrumental in allowing the country to benefit from international trade and tourism.

## Transportation by Air in Canada

Transportation by air in Canada is an integral part of the country's economy and is responsible for the rapid growth of tourism and business in many regions. Canada is the world's second largest country in terms of area and its vast geography makes air transportation a critical component of the nation's transportation system. Air travel in Canada is served by over 100 airlines, many of them offering domestic and international flights, as well as a range of charter services.

Copyrighted Material

Canada's air transportation system is made up of several major airports, as well as a vast network of regional and smaller airports throughout the country. The largest airports in Canada are Toronto Pearson International Airport, Vancouver International Airport, Calgary International Airport, and Montreal-Trudeau International Airport. These airports are the hub for the majority of international flights to and from Canada, and they also serve as major hubs for domestic flights throughout the country.

The Canadian government has invested heavily in the development of air transportation infrastructure in the country, with a focus on safety and security. Airport security has been increased in recent years, and all airports in Canada are equipped with the latest in security technology. Additionally, the government has invested

Copyrighted Material

in the modernization of air traffic control systems, as well as the construction of new airports and the expansion of existing ones.

In addition to commercial passenger travel, air transportation in Canada is also responsible for the transportation of goods and services, with goods and services being shipped via cargo planes to various destinations. The goods and services being shipped via air transportation vary depending on the region, with goods such as fresh produce, electronics, and medical supplies being transported all across the country.

Air transportation in Canada is an important part of the nation's economy, with the majority of the population relying on air transportation for both business and pleasure. Air transportation is responsible for the growth of tourism in many regions, as well as the transportation of goods and

Copyrighted Material

services across the country. In addition, air transportation is necessary for the efficient and safe transportation of people, goods, and services, making it an integral part of the Canadian economy.

Overall, air transportation in Canada is an essential component of the country's economy. The government has invested heavily in the development of air transportation infrastructure in the country, with a focus on safety and security. Additionally, air transportation is responsible for the transportation of goods and services, as well as the growth of tourism in many regions. As a result, air transportation is an important part of the Canadian economy and is necessary for the efficient and safe transportation of people, goods, and services.

Copyrighted Material

## Transportation by Road in Canada

Canada has an extensive network of roads and highways that span the country from coast to coast. The Trans-Canada Highway is the longest national highway in the world, stretching over 8,000 km from St. John's, Newfoundland in the east to Victoria, British Columbia in the west. It passes through 10 provinces and is a major route for tourists and freight traffic.

Other major highways in Canada include the Queen Elizabeth Way, which connects Toronto to Niagara Falls, the Yellowhead Highway, which runs between Manitoba and Alberta, and the Trans-Canada Highway, which links all of the provinces.

In addition to these major highways, there are thousands of smaller roads and

Copyrighted Material

highways that connect towns, cities, and remote areas across the country. These roads are maintained by provincial and municipal governments and are often the only way to access more remote regions.

Public transportation by road is also available in Canada, including buses, trains, and ferries. In some areas, public transportation is integrated with other forms of public transportation, such as light rail and subway systems.

Most Canadians rely on cars for their daily transportation needs. Canada has one of the highest car ownership rates in the world, with over 85% of households owning at least one vehicle

In recent years, the Canadian government has been investing in new technologies to improve road safety and reduce congestion. These include intelligent transportation systems, which use sensors to monitor

Copyrighted Material

traffic flow, as well as automated vehicles and connected cars that can communicate with each other to reduce collisions.

Overall, transportation by road in Canada is an important part of the country's transportation infrastructure. It is a safe and efficient way to travel, and it helps to connect people and businesses to each other.

The Canadian government continues to invest in new technologies and infrastructure to ensure that roads are safe and efficient for everyone who uses them.

## Transportation by Rail in Canada

Rail transportation in Canada is a very important part of the country's transportation network. It is used to transport people and goods, and is an

Copyrighted Material

efficient and cost-effective way to move people and goods across the country. The Canadian railway system is made up of both public and private railways, and is regulated by the federal government.

The Canadian railway system is the longest in the world, with over 46,000 kilometers of track. It is a highly efficient way to move people and goods from one part of the country to another, and is the preferred mode of transportation for many businesses across Canada. The railway system is also a major provider of jobs in Canada, with over 70,000 people employed in the industry.

The Canadian railway system is divided into two main networks: the national railway network and the regional railway network. The national railway network is composed of the Canadian National Railway, Canadian Pacific Railway, and VIA Rail Canada. These

Copyrighted Material

companies operate on a national scale, transporting people and goods across the country. The regional railway network is made up of smaller, regional railways, which provide local and regional passenger service. Rail transportation is an important part of Canada's transportation system. It is a safe, reliable, and efficient way to move people and goods

across the country. It is also an environmentally-friendly option, as it emits fewer emissions than other forms of transportation. Additionally, rail transportation is an affordable way to travel, making it a popular choice for many Canadians.

Rail transportation in Canada is an important part of the country's transportation infrastructure. It is used to transport people and goods across the country, and provides efficient and

Copyrighted Material

cost-effective transportation solutions for businesses and individuals alike. By investing in rail infrastructure, Canada is investing in its future, ensuring that it has a safe and reliable transportation network for generations to come.

The Canadian railway system is a major contributor to the country's economy, and is an essential part of Canada's infrastructure. It is an important part of the country's transportation network, and is an efficient and cost-effective way to move people and goods. By investing in rail infrastructure and continuing to support the railway system, Canada is ensuring that it has a safe and reliable transportation network for the future.

Rail transportation in Canada is an important part of the country's transportation infrastructure. It is an

Copyrighted Material

efficient and cost-effective way to move people and goods across the country, and is an environmentally-friendly option for transportation. With continued investment in rail infrastructure and support for the railway system, Canada is ensuring that it has a safe and reliable transportation network for the future.

Rail transportation in Canada is an important part of the country's transportation infrastructure. It is an efficient and cost-effective way to move people and goods across the country, and is an environmentally-friendly option for transportation. With continued investment in rail infrastructure and support for the railway system, Canada is ensuring that it has a safe and reliable transportation network for the future.

Rail transportation in Canada is an important part of the country's

Copyrighted Material

transportation infrastructure. It is an efficient and cost-effective way to move people and goods across the country, and is an environmentally-friendly option for transportation. The Canadian railway system is a major contributor to the country's economy, and is an essential part of Canada's infrastructure. By investing in rail infrastructure and continuing to support the railway system, Canada is ensuring that it has a safe and reliable transportation network for the future.

Copyrighted Material

## Chapter 4

# Accommodations in Canada

Accommodations in Canada are some of the best in the world. From luxurious five-star resorts to cozy bed and breakfasts, there is an accommodation option to suit every budget and travel style. Canada is home to a wide variety of accommodations, from hotels and motels to hostels and camping grounds. Whether you're looking for a place to stay for a weekend getaway or an extended stay, Canada has something to offer you.

No matter where you choose to stay, you can be sure to find a variety of amenities and services. Many hotels offer swimming pools, fitness centers, and on-site restaurants. Hostels and bed and breakfasts often

Copyrighted Material

provide cozy and comfortable rooms with basic amenities. Whether you're looking for a place to sleep or a luxurious experience, Canada has something to offer everyone.

When booking accommodations in Canada, it's important to research the different types of accommodations available and the amenities each offers. Be sure to read reviews and compare prices to ensure you're getting the most value for your money. Additionally, it's important to consider the location of the accommodation and how close it is to the attractions you'd like to visit.

Accommodations in Canada offer visitors a variety of options for a comfortable and memorable stay. With so many different types of accommodation available, you're sure to find something that suits your needs and budget.

Copyrighted Material

So, what are you waiting for? Start exploring Canada's accommodations today!

Canada is a popular destination for travelers, and it offers a wide variety of accommodations to suit every budget and style. From luxurious hotels and resorts to cozy bed and breakfasts and hostels, there is something for everyone in Canada. In this article, we will explore the different types of hotels and accommodations available in Canada and the features they offer.

Hotels are one of the most popular accommodation choices in Canada. Hotels range in size and style, from large international chains to boutique hotels. Most hotels offer a variety of amenities such as pools, fitness centers, restaurants, and bars. Many hotels also offer free Wi-Fi, free parking, and other services such as room service and laundry facilities. Hotels are a great option for business travelers and those

Copyrighted Material

looking for a comfortable and convenient place to stay.

Bed and Breakfasts (B&Bs) are also popular in Canada. B&Bs offer a home-like atmosphere and often feature unique touches like homemade breakfasts and a friendly host. B&Bs are usually located in residential areas and are a great option for travelers looking for a more intimate and cozy experience.

Copyrighted Material

## Hostels Accommodations in Canada

Canada is home to some of the most beautiful natural scenery in the world and attracts tourists from all over the globe. For those travelers looking for an affordable and unique way to experience the country, hostels are an excellent option. Hostels provide budget-friendly, social accommodations for those who want to travel on the cheap.

The hostels in Canada vary in size and amenities, but all provide a safe, comfortable place to stay. Most hostels are equipped with shared living spaces, kitchens, and bathrooms, and some offer additional amenities such as Wi-Fi, laundry facilities, and bike rental services. Hostels also offer a wide variety of activities, from organized hikes and camping trips to kayaking and skiing.

Copyrighted Material

For those looking for a more private experience, there are plenty of private rooms available in hostels across the country. These rooms come in both single and double occupancy, and are typically equipped with a private bathroom and kitchenette.

No matter where you choose to stay in Canada, hostels are a great way to save money on your accommodations. Not only are they affordable, but they offer a unique and social atmosphere that you won't find in other types of lodging. So whether you're looking to explore the wilds of Canada or experience

Its vibrant cities, hostels are an ideal place to stay.

Copyrighted Material

## Camping Accommodations in Canada

When it comes to camping in Canada, there are plenty of accommodation options to choose from. From rustic camping tents and cabins to luxury RV resorts and hotels, campers of all kinds can find a perfect fit for their vacation.

For those looking for a more traditional camping experience, Canada offers plenty of options. Whether you prefer camping in the wilderness or in a campground, you can easily find a spot to pitch your tent or park your RV. Popular places to camp include provincial and national parks, where you

Copyrighted Material

can find plenty of hiking trails, picnic spots, and scenic views.

For those who prefer a more luxurious camping experience, there are plenty of RV parks and resorts available. These places offer a variety of amenities, including full hook-ups, swimming pools, and on-site restaurants. Many of these resorts also offer activities such as kayaking and fishing, as well as special events like movie nights and BBQs.

Finally, for those looking for a unique place to stay, Canada also offers a number of cabins, yurts, and lodges. These accommodations are usually located in remote areas, offering a great opportunity to get away from it all and enjoy the peace and quiet of nature. Plus, many of these accommodations come with amenities like hot tubs and fire pits, providing a cozy atmosphere to spend your evenings.

Copyrighted Material

No matter what type of camping accommodations you're looking for, Canada has something to offer. With its diverse terrain, various accommodation options, and breathtaking views, Canada is the perfect place to spend your next camping vacation.

Copyrighted Material

## Chapter 5

## canada Food

Food in Canada is a reflection of the country's diverse and multicultural population. From traditional Aboriginal dishes to the latest fusion cuisine, there is something for everyone. Canadians enjoy a wide variety of dishes from all over the world, and many of them have become part of the national cuisine. From French-Canadian poutine to Asian-inspired dim sum, Canadian food is as diverse as its population. From coast to coast to coast, Canadians have access to a wide variety of fresh and locally grown produce, seafood, and meats. As a result, Canadians have created a unique culinary landscape that celebrates both local and international flavours.

Copyrighted Material

Canada has a long history of embracing multicultural cuisine, with each region developing its own unique flavours. In the east, there is a strong French-Canadian influence, while in the west, there is an abundance of Asian and First Nations cuisine. In the north, Inuit culture has impacted the cuisine, while in the south, the flavours of the United States are evident. No matter where you are in Canada, you can find a variety of delicious foods to enjoy.

Food in Canada is a reflection of the country's diverse and multicultural population. From traditional Aboriginal dishes to the latest fusion cuisine, there is something for everyone. Canadians enjoy a wide variety of dishes from all over the world, and many of them have become part of the national cuisine. From

Copyrighted Material

French-Canadian poutine to Asian-inspired dim sum, Canadian food is as diverse as its population. From coast to coast to coast, Canadians have access to a wide variety of fresh and locally grown produce, seafood, and meats. As a result, Canadians have created a unique culinary landscape that celebrates both local and international flavours.

Canada has a long history of embracing multicultural cuisine, with each region developing its own unique flavours. In the east, there is a strong French-Canadian influence, while in the west, there is an abundance of Asian and First Nations cuisine. In the north, Inuit culture has impacted the cuisine, while in the south, the flavours of the United States are evident. No matter where you are in Canada, you can find a variety of delicious foods to enjoy.

Copyrighted Material

## Traditional Cuisine

Canada has a unique cuisine that draws from its history. Traditional Canadian foods are a combination of French, British, First Nations, and other influences. Dishes often include wild game, such as moose and deer, as well as seafood from both the Atlantic and Pacific coasts.

Poutine is one of the most popular dishes in Canada. It consists of french fries, cheese curds, and gravy. It originated in Quebec,

Copyrighted Material

but has now become popular across the country.

Another popular dish is tourtière, a meat pie that is usually made with pork, beef, veal, or game. It is usually served with condiments such as ketchup, mustard, pickles, and hot sauce.

Pea soup is another traditional Canadian dish. It is made with split peas, carrots, onions, and bacon. It is usually served with fresh-baked rolls.

Maple syrup is an important ingredient in many Canadian dishes. Maple syrup is usually used to sweeten desserts, such as maple tarts and maple syrup pie, as well as beverages like maple tea.

BeaverTails are a popular snack. They are fried dough pastries that are often topped with sweet or savoury ingredients.

Copyrighted Material

Canadian cuisine also includes a variety of smoked and cured meats, such as bacon and smoked salmon. These are often served with pancakes or eggs and are a popular breakfast dish.

Canada is also known for its fresh seafood. Lobster, crab, and mussels are some of the most popular seafood dishes.

Overall, Canada has a diverse and flavorful cuisine that reflects its history and cultural influences. From wild game and seafood to sweet treats and savoury dishes, Canadian cuisine has something to please everyone.

## Popular Dishes

Canada is known for having a diverse and unique cuisine that is reflective of its many cultures and traditions. From poutine to bannock, there is no shortage of delicious dishes to try. Poutine is a classic Canadian dish consisting of french fries, cheese curds

Copyrighted Material

and gravy. Bannock is a traditional Indigenous dish made of flour, water, salt, and baking powder that is often cooked over an open fire. Tourtière is a French-Canadian meat pie made with ground pork, beef, or game, potatoes, and spices. Butter tarts are small pastries filled with a mixture of butter, sugar, syrup, and eggs. Maple syrup is a quintessential Canadian ingredient, and is used in a variety of dishes, from desserts to savory dishes. Baked beans are a popular side dish and often include bacon, maple syrup, and molasses. Fish and chips is another popular dish, made with fresh fish that is battered and fried, and served with chips. Each region of Canada has its own unique cuisine, and is a great place to explore different flavors and dishes.

No matter what type of cuisine you are looking for, Canada has something for

Copyrighted Material

everyone. From hearty comfort food to fine dining, there is no shortage of delicious dishes to try.

## Restaurants

Canada is home to a diverse range of food cultures, with many different types of restaurants to choose from. From fine dining to casual eateries, there's something for everyone in Canada.

Copyrighted Material

Fine Dining: Canada has some of the best fine dining establishments in the world. From traditional French cuisine to modern fusion dishes, there's something for everyone. Popular fine dining restaurants include Toqué!, Hawksworth Restaurant, and Langdon Hall.

Casual Dining: Canada is full of casual dining options, from cozy cafes to lively bars. Popular restaurants include The Keg, Jack Astor's, and Milestones.

Seafood: Canada is known for its fresh seafood, and there are many restaurants that specialize in seafood dishes. Popular seafood restaurants include The Fish Shack, Catch 122, and Rodney's Oyster House.

Ethnic Cuisine: Canada is home to many different ethnic cuisines, from Chinese to Indian to Middle Eastern. Popular ethnic restaurants include FUSIAN, Kinka Izakaya, and Rangoli.

Copyrighted Material

Fast Food: Canada also has plenty of fast food options, from traditional burgers and fries to specialty items. Popular fast food restaurants include McDonald's, A&W, and Tim Hort

Whether you're looking for a fine dining experience or a quick bite, Canada has something for everyone.

Copyrighted Material

## Chapter 6

## Safety in Canada

Safety in Canada is a priority for the government and the people. The country has a variety of laws and regulations in place to ensure a safe environment for its citizens. Canada has some of the lowest crime rates in the world, and its citizens consistently report feeling safe in their communities.

The Canadian government has invested heavily in public safety initiatives, such as police services, emergency response services, and crime prevention efforts. Canada has also developed a number of programs to address issues such as domestic violence, child abuse, and bullying. Canada also has a variety of laws in place to protect the rights of individuals, such as the Canadian Charter of Rights and Freedoms.

Copyrighted Material

The Canadian government works closely with local law enforcement agencies to ensure the safety of its citizens. Police officers are trained to respond to a variety of situations, and their presence in communities is often seen as a deterrent to crime. Canada also has a variety of laws and regulations in place to protect the safety of its citizens. These include laws on firearms, self-defense, and property protection.

Canada is also a leader in the development of innovative safety technologies. These include surveillance systems, biometrics, and even drones that can be used to monitor public spaces. There is also an emphasis on education and public outreach to help citizens understand the importance of personal safety and to teach them how to protect themselves in public.

Copyrighted Material

Overall, safety in Canada is a priority for the government and its citizens. The country has a variety of laws and regulations in place to ensure a safe environment for its citizens, and it invests in public safety initiatives to ensure that everyone feels safe and secure in their communities.

## Security

Security in Canada is a priority for the government and its citizens. The government has implemented a number of laws and regulations to ensure that security is maintained in the country.

The Canadian Security Intelligence Service (CSIS) is the federal agency responsible for

Copyrighted Material

national security. It collects and analyzes intelligence on threats to the country and provides advice to the Canadian government. It is also responsible for conducting investigations, making arrests, and gathering intelligence on terrorist activities. CSIS works with other law enforcement agencies, such as the Royal Canadian Mounted Police (RCMP) and the Canadian Border Services Agency, to ensure the security of Canada and its citizens.

The government has also implemented a number of measures to prevent the smuggling of weapons and explosives into the country. The Customs and Excise Act gives the Canada Border Services Agency the authority to search and seize goods that may be related to terrorism or other illegal activities. The Security of Canada Information Sharing Act allows the sharing of information between federal departments

Copyrighted Material

and agencies, as well as certain provincial and municipal organizations, in order to better detect and prevent terrorism and other threats.

The government has also established the National Security Program, which is designed to ensure that Canada is prepared to respond to potential national security threats and emergencies. This program includes the

Canadian Security Establishment (CSE), which is responsible for electronic surveillance and cyber security. The CSE works with other departments and agencies to monitor and protect Canada's cyber networks, as well as investigate and analyze cyber threats.

Overall, the Canadian government takes security very seriously and has implemented a number of measures to ensure that Canada remains safe and secure.

Copyrighted Material

## Crime

Crime in Canada is a serious issue, and the country has experienced a significant increase in crime over the past two decades. In 2018, the crime rate in Canada rose to its highest rate since 1998, with a total of 1,951,678 criminal incidents reported by police.

Violent crime is the fastest growing type of crime in Canada, with the number of incidents rising by 11% between 2017 and 2018. In 2018, there were 22,948 homicides, attempted homicides, and related offences reported to police, a 5%

Copyrighted Material

increase from 2017. Robbery and break and enter offences also rose significantly, with the latter increasing by 6%.

Drug-related offences continue to be the most common type of crime in Canada, accounting for 14% of all reported criminal incidents in 2018. The number of drug-related offences has increased steadily since 2014, with a total of 276,845 reported in 2018.

Property crime is the second most common type of crime in Canada, accounting for nearly 40% of all reported criminal incidents in 2018. This includes theft and theft of motor vehicles, which accounted for 15% and 5% of all reported incidents respectively.

Overall, crime in Canada is a complex and multifaceted issue. The government and

Copyrighted Material

provincial and territorial authorities have implemented a variety of initiatives to address the issue, such as the National Crime Prevention Strategy and the National Action Plan on Crime Prevention. However, it is clear that more needs to be done to reduce crime rates in Canada.

## Natural Threats

Natural threats are an unfortunate reality of life in Canada. From earthquakes and floods to landslides and wildfires, these events have the potential to cause significant destruction, loss of life, and disruption to the lives of Canadians and their communities.

Earthquakes are a common natural threat in Canada, and can be particularly destructive depending on the magnitude of the quake.

Copyrighted Material

Earthquakes occur when tectonic plates move, creating pressure and friction that can cause the surface of the earth to move or shake. Earthquakes can also cause tsunamis, which can lead to coastal flooding and destruction.

Floods are a common natural threat in Canada, especially in the spring and summer months. When heavy rains fall, rivers and streams can overflow, leading to flooding in nearby areas. Floods can cause destruction to homes and public infrastructure, as well as contaminate water sources.

Landslides are a natural threat caused by erosion, and can occur when there is a sudden change in the terrain, such as during a large storm or an earthquake. Landslides can cause significant destruction to property

Copyrighted Material

and infrastructure, as well as disrupt transportation routes.

Wildfires are a natural threat in Canada, particularly during the summer months when the weather is dry and hot.

Wildfires can cause significant destruction to homes and public infrastructure, as well as disrupt transportation routes. Wildfires also create air pollution and can affect people's health.

Natural threats can have a serious impact on Canadians and their communities. It is important to be aware of the risks, take the necessary precautions, and be prepared for the worst.

By understanding the potential impacts of natural threats, Canadians can be better prepared to protect themselves, their families, and their communities.

Copyrighted Material

From earthquakes and floods to landslides and wildfires, natural threats are an unfortunate part of life in Canada. By understanding the risks and taking the necessary precautions, Canadians can be better prepared to protect themselves and their communities in the event of a natural disaster.

Copyrighted Material

# Conclusion

Canada is a great place to explore and experience the beauty of nature, culture, and history. With its diverse landscapes and activities, there is something for everyone to enjoy in Canada. From the majestic Rocky Mountains to the rugged coastlines of the East, and the unique cities and towns in between, Canada offers a unique and unforgettable experience for travelers. With its friendly and welcoming people, Canada is sure to make any trip a memorable one.

Overall, Canada is an amazing destination for travelers who are looking for adventure, culture, and relaxation. With its stunning landscapes, bustling cities, and unique attractions, Canada is a must-visit destination for those who want to experience the best of what the country has to offer.

Copyrighted Material

No matter what your travel style is, Canada has something to offer everyone. Whether you're looking for a relaxing getaway, an exciting adventure, or something in between, Canada is sure to provide you with a memorable and enjoyable experience.

Canada is a wonderful destination for any traveler, no matter their style or interests. With its stunning landscapes, vibrant cities, and endless activities, it is a perfect destination for anyone looking to explore, relax, and experience the best of what Canada has to offer.

Happy travels!

.

Copyrighted Material